# The Shepherds' Story

Retold by Carol Watson

Illustrations by
Toni Goffe

A LION BOOK

Oxford · Batavia · Sydney

All around the little town of
Bethlehem there were fields where
flocks of sheep grazed.

Shepherds watched over the sheep,
keeping them safe from wolves and
making sure they did not stray or
get lost.

One cold night out on the hillside,
the shepherds sat warming
themselves by the fire.

"The town is very crowded tonight,"
said one. "There is nowhere left for
any visitors to stay."

"Yes," said another. "I'm glad to be
out here where it's quiet and
peaceful."

The shepherds sat for hours in the stillness of the night watching over their flocks and chatting happily to each other.

Suddenly an incredible brightness lit up the dark sky.

"What's that?" cried a shepherd.

They all looked up in wonder and amazement.

There shining above them was one of God's angels.

The shepherds were very frightened.

"Do not be afraid," said the angel. "I have come to tell you good news which will bring joy to all the world.

"Today, in Bethlehem, a baby was born. He is the Saviour – God's promised King. Go and see him. You will find the baby wrapped up tightly, lying in a manger."

Then, all at once, the whole sky was
full of angels. They were singing
together praising and thanking God
for his gift to the world.

"Glory to God in heaven," they
sang, "and peace on earth to those
who love him."

The shepherds could not believe
their eyes. Then, just as suddenly as
they had come, the angels
disappeared.

The sky was dark again and
everything was quiet.

"Come on, let's go into Bethlehem,"
said one shepherd. "We must
see what this is all about."

So the shepherds set off across the fields and made their way into the sleeping town.

"The angel said the baby was in a manger," they whispered among themselves.

"He must have been born in a stable somewhere."

The streets of Bethlehem were quiet
now. Everyone was sleeping
soundly after the busy day.

The shepherds moved quietly
through the town, searching for the
new-born child. They looked in every
stable they could find.

Then one of the shepherds had an idea.

"We haven't tried the cave behind that inn," he said. "The innkeeper sometimes puts his animals there."

So, at last, they came to the inn, and found the cave close by.

The shepherds peeped into the cave.

Sitting quietly on the hay, among all the animals, they saw Mary and Joseph.

And there, lying in the manger, was a tiny, new-born baby boy.

Just as the angel had said, the baby was wrapped up tightly to keep him safe and warm in the cold night air.

As soon as they saw the child, the shepherds knelt down and worshipped him.

"We saw an angel in the sky," they said to Joseph. "He told us that this baby will bring great joy to all the world. He is the Saviour – God's promised King."

Then the shepherds told Mary and Joseph everything that had happened that night, out on the dark hillside.

Mary listened carefully as she held the baby Jesus in her arms. She knew that she would never forget all the wonderful things the angel had said.

Afterwards the shepherds hurried back to their sheep.

They were very happy that God had sent an angel to speak to them. As they ran through the fields, the shepherds sang hymns of joy and praise for all that had happened.

Text copyright © 1990 Carol Watson
Illustrations copyright © 1990 Toni Goffe

Published by
**Lion Publishing plc**
Sandy Lane West, Oxford,
England
ISBN 0 7459 1866 2
**Lion Publishing Corporation**
1705 Hubbard Avenue, Batavia,
Illinois 60510, USA
ISBN 0 7459 1866 2
**Albatross Books Pty Ltd**
PO Box 320, Sutherland, NSW 2232,
Australia
ISBN 0 7324 0174 7

First edition 1990
Reprinted 1991

Printed and bound in Singapore

This book
belongs to

........................................................

# First Dictionary

**Words:**

Alison Niblo
and
Janet De Saulles

**Consultant: Betty Root**

**Pictures:**

**Kim Woolley**

## Contents

Note to the reader

"Doing" words, such as "**walking**," are printed in **gray**.
These words tell you about what is happening in the pictures.

SMITHMARK

# Pets

fish

fishbowl

fish food

walking

puppy

dog

bone

doghouse

bowl

parakeet

perch

birdseed

hamster

guinea pig

holding

stroking

cat

gerbil

basket

kitten

hutch

cage

mouse

rabbit

water bottle

straw

shavings

# Creepy critters

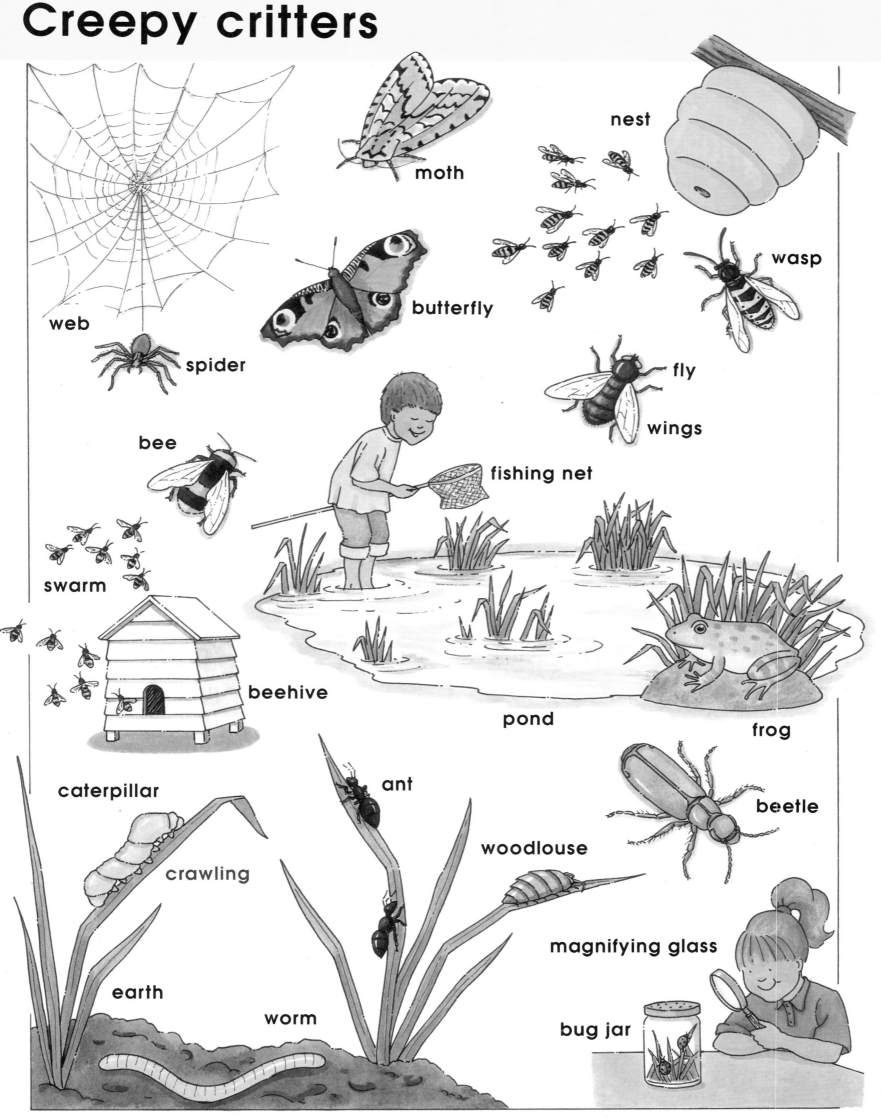

web

moth

nest

wasp

spider

butterfly

fly

wings

bee

fishing net

swarm

beehive

pond

frog

caterpillar

ant

beetle

crawling

woodlouse

earth

worm

magnifying glass

bug jar

3

# At the wildlife park

monkey

scratching

elephant

gorilla

rhinoceros

giraffe

zebra

tiger

cheetah

running

lion

dolphin

kangaroo

snake

polar bear

shark

penguin

seal

octopus

turtle

crocodile

eel

hippopotamus

water hole

4

# In the country

woods

hill

truck

stile

sheep

combine

lamb

farm

field

stable

barn

gate

horse

sty

farmer

hen

tractor

pig

orchard

bull

goose

hedge

duck

cow

duck pond

stream

5

# Fun outdoors

slide

falling

ropes

jungle gym

climbing

playground

swings

caravan

campsite

tent

helmet

pads

skateboard

soccer

kicking

ramp

bat

throwing

catching

basketball

picnic

jumping

roller skates

water fight

splashing

paddling pool

6

# At the amusement park

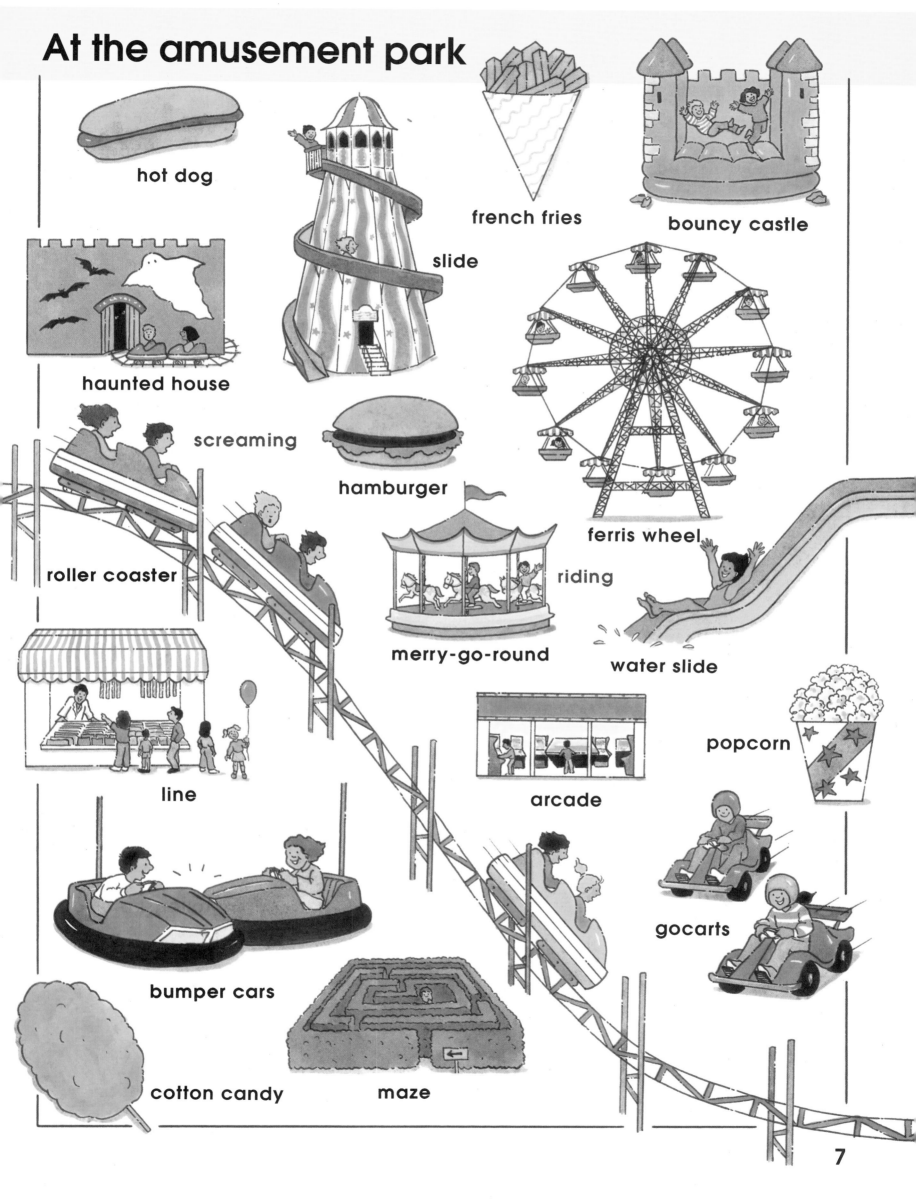

hot dog

french fries

bouncy castle

slide

haunted house

screaming

hamburger

ferris wheel

roller coaster

merry-go-round

riding

water slide

line

arcade

popcorn

bumper cars

maze

gocarts

cotton candy

7

# At the beach

bowling

goggles

snorkel

ice cream

wet suit

beach mat

kiosk

crab

flippers

starfish

pier

waterskiing

life guard

seaweed

paddling

digging

water wings

inflatable ring

shovel

making

moat

bucket

sand

pebbles

sand castle

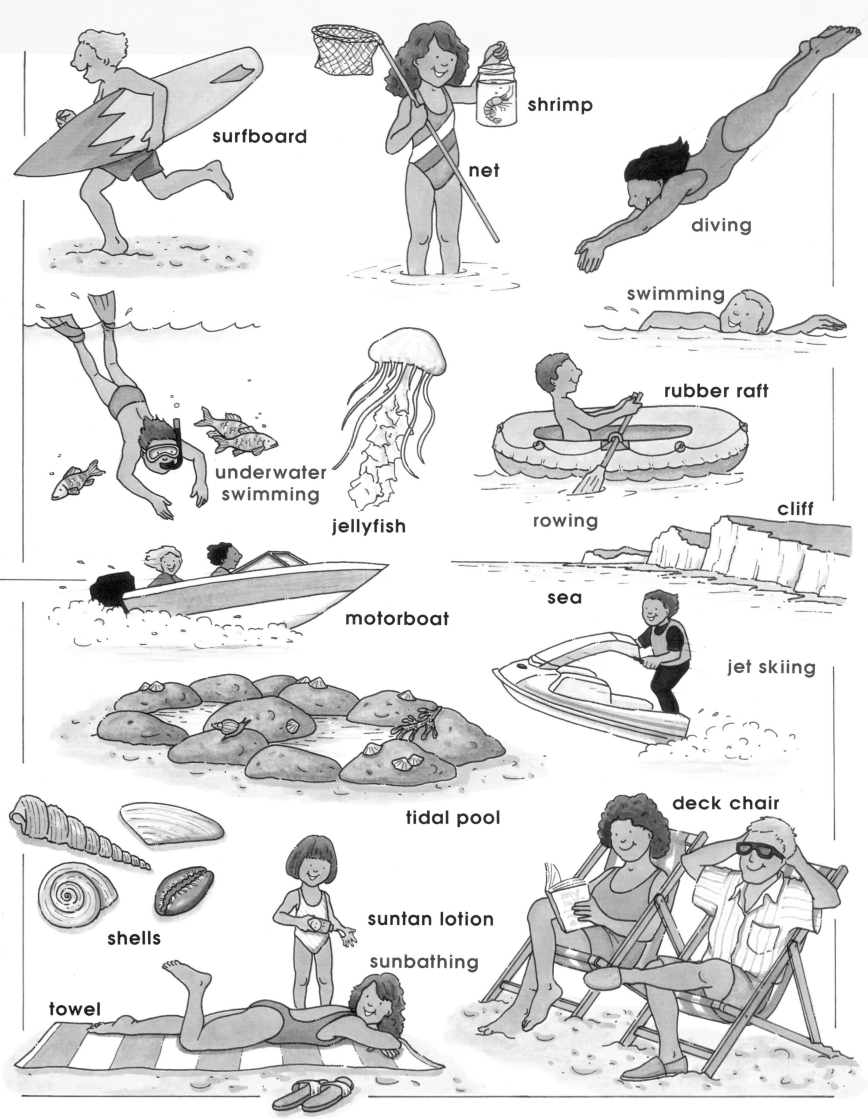

surfboard

shrimp

net

diving

swimming

rubber raft

underwater swimming

jellyfish

rowing

cliff

motorboat

sea

jet skiing

tidal pool

deck chair

shells

suntan lotion

sunbathing

towel

# Buildings

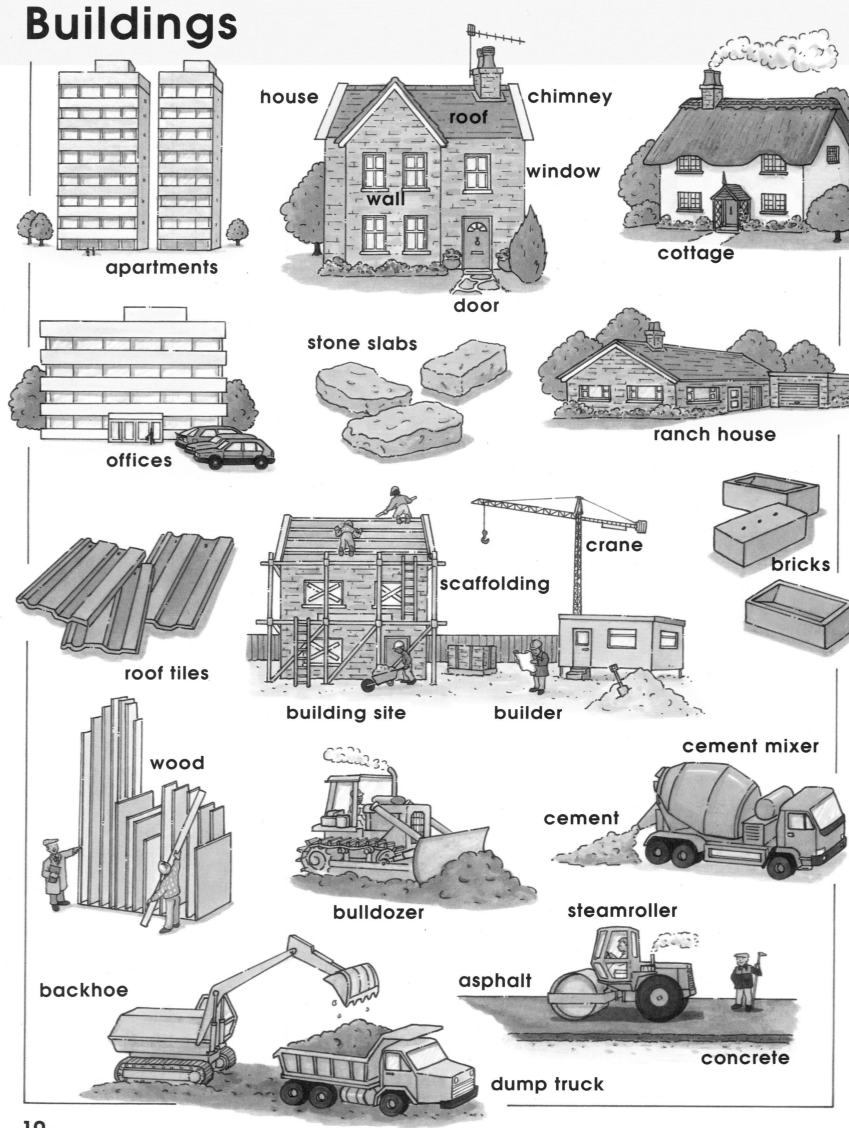

apartments

house

chimney

roof

window

wall

door

cottage

offices

stone slabs

ranch house

roof tiles

scaffolding

crane

bricks

building site

builder

wood

bulldozer

cement mixer

cement

steamroller

backhoe

asphalt

dump truck

concrete

10

# On the move

helicopter

rotor blades

airport

hot-air balloon

airplane

runway

flying

truck

train station

unloading

motorcycle

train

bicycle

passengers

driving

driver

car

van

minibus

bus

taxi

cruise liner

ferryboat

sailing

hovercraft

sailboat

# In the street

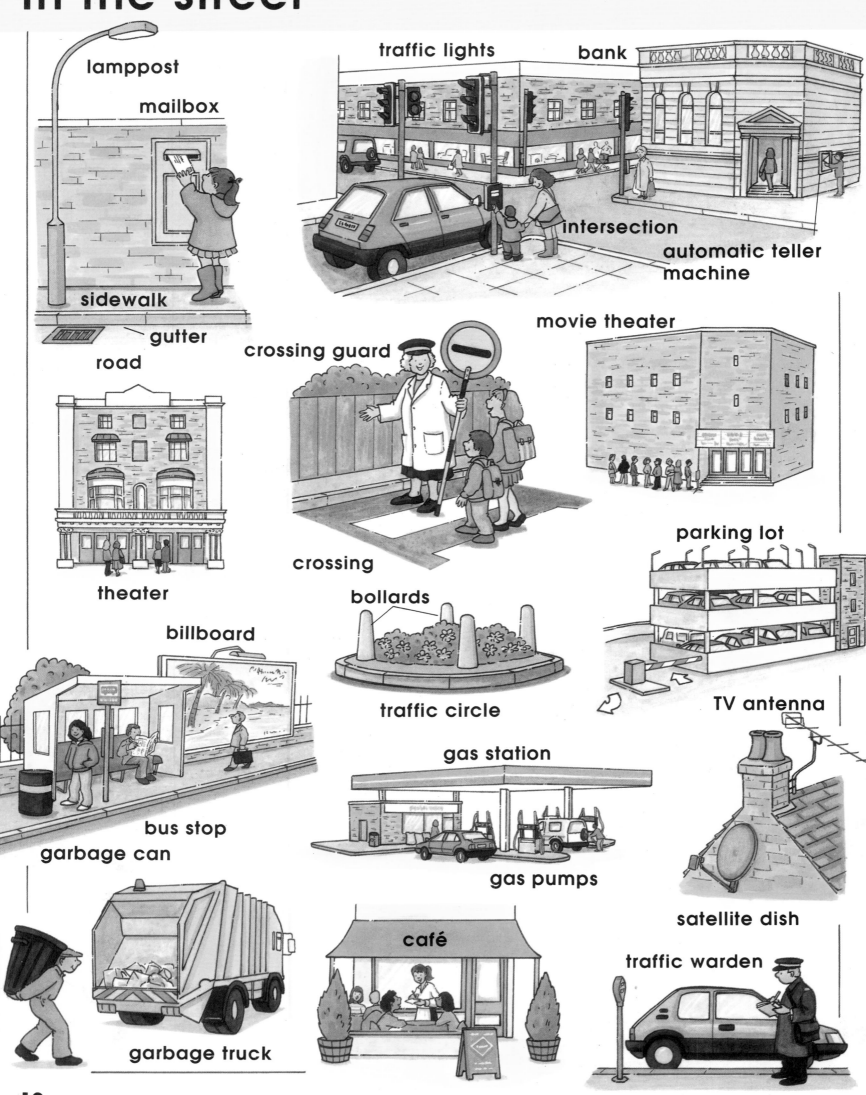

lamppost

mailbox

traffic lights

bank

sidewalk

gutter

road

crossing guard

movie theater

intersection

automatic teller machine

theater

crossing

parking lot

billboard

bollards

traffic circle

TV antenna

gas station

bus stop

garbage can

gas pumps

satellite dish

café

traffic warden

garbage truck

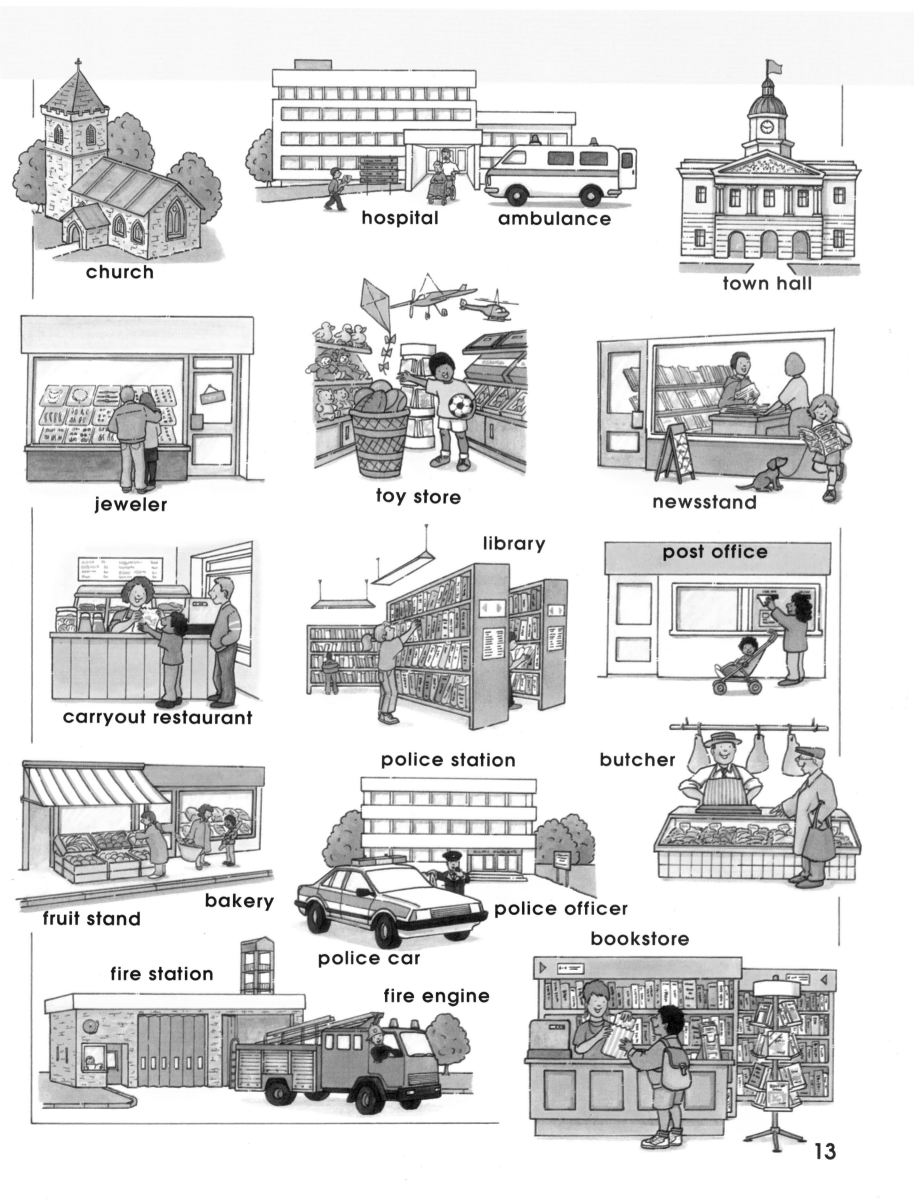

church

hospital     ambulance

town hall

jeweler

toy store

newsstand

library

post office

carryout restaurant

police station     butcher

fruit stand

bakery

police officer

bookstore

fire station

police car

fire engine

13

# At the supermarket

shelves

rice and pasta

shopping cart

delicatessen

checkout clerk

cash register

bar code

bread and cakes

checkout

fruit and vegetables

yogurt

sour cream

dairy food

cheese

milk

money

receipt

household items

frozen food

label

canned food

# Cooking

wooden spoon

stirring

mixing bowl

flour

frosting

powdered sugar

baking tray

recipe

oven

ingredients

spatula

tasting

cooking

pie

eggs

weighing

cookies

scale

apron

chopping

margarine

rolling

rolling pin

sugar

pastry cutter

# At home

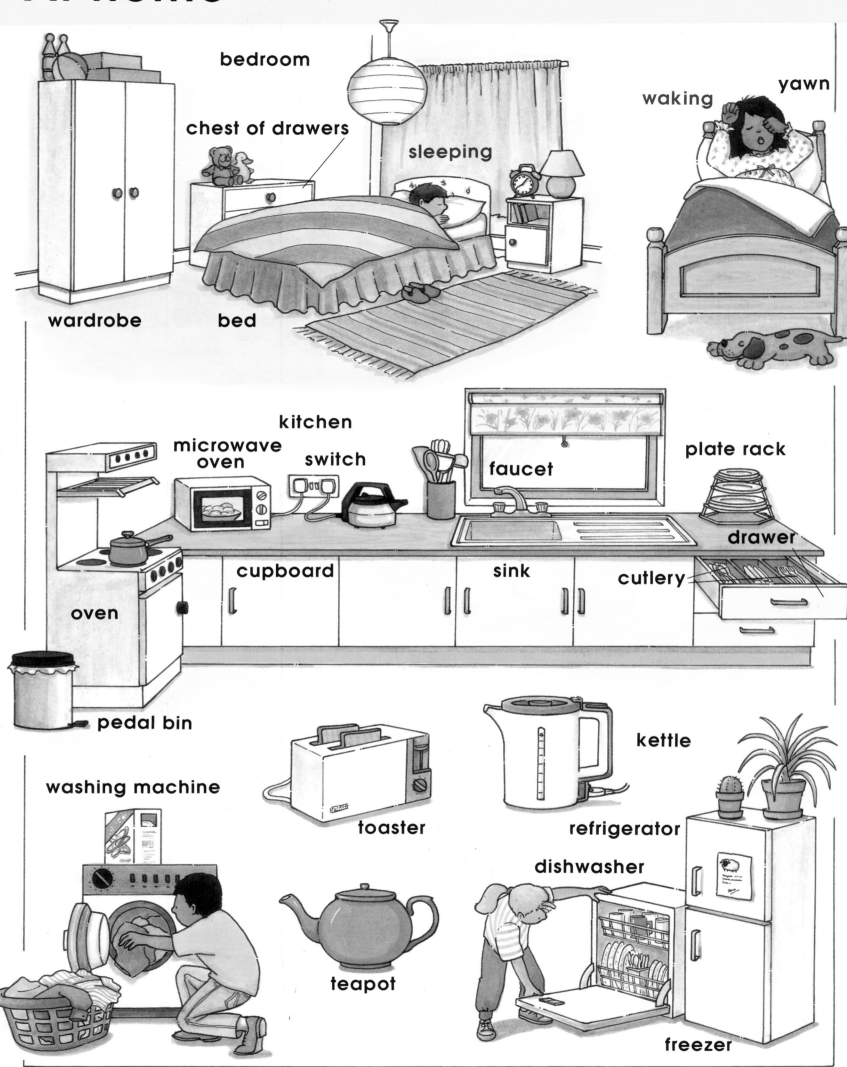

bedroom

chest of drawers

sleeping

waking

yawn

wardrobe

bed

kitchen

microwave oven

switch

faucet

plate rack

oven

cupboard

sink

cutlery

drawer

pedal bin

washing machine

toaster

kettle

refrigerator

dishwasher

teapot

freezer

mirror

brushing

bathroom

washing

soap

bubbles

sink

toilet

bathtub

upstairs

answering machine

front door

telephone

hall

downstairs

listening

music system

armchair

living room

garage

watching

shed

television

backyard

video recorder

sofa

17

# My family

young  younger  youngest

old  older  oldest

mommy  daddy

sister

brother

parents  son  daughter

uncle  aunt

nephew  niece

cousin

grandma

baby

grandpa  grandchild

twins

triplets

# Party time

wrapping paper

birthday cards

presents

playing

happy birthday!

streamers

balloons

candles

blowing

birthday cake

happy

magician

prize

dance

dancing

drinking

eating

full!

19

# About myself

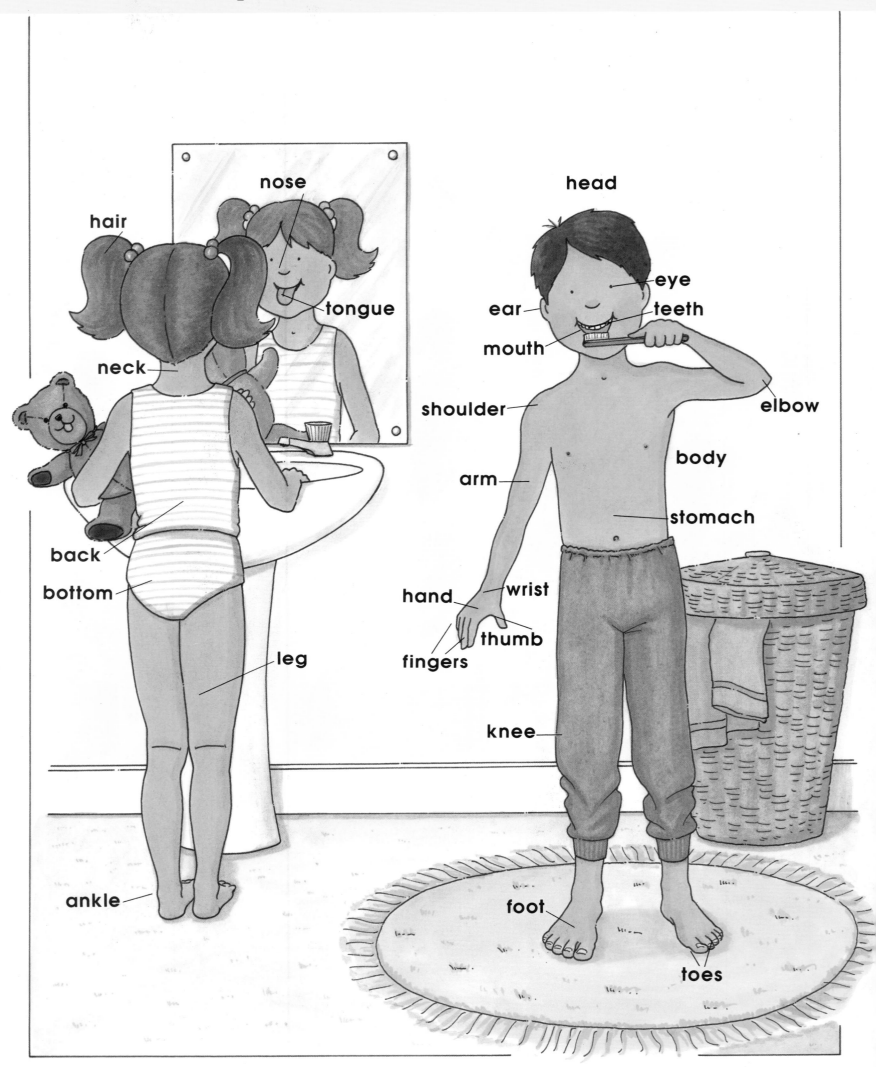

hair

nose

tongue

neck

back

bottom

ankle

leg

head

eye

ear

teeth

mouth

shoulder

elbow

body

arm

stomach

hand

wrist

thumb

fingers

knee

foot

toes

# Feeling sick

adhesive bandage

cut

headache

stomachache

pills

doctor's office

nurse

patient

waiting room

doctor

cold

sneeze

sore throat

thermometer

medicine

stethoscope

antiseptic cream

bandage

sling

dentist

drill

crutches

broken leg

plaster cast

21

# Clothes

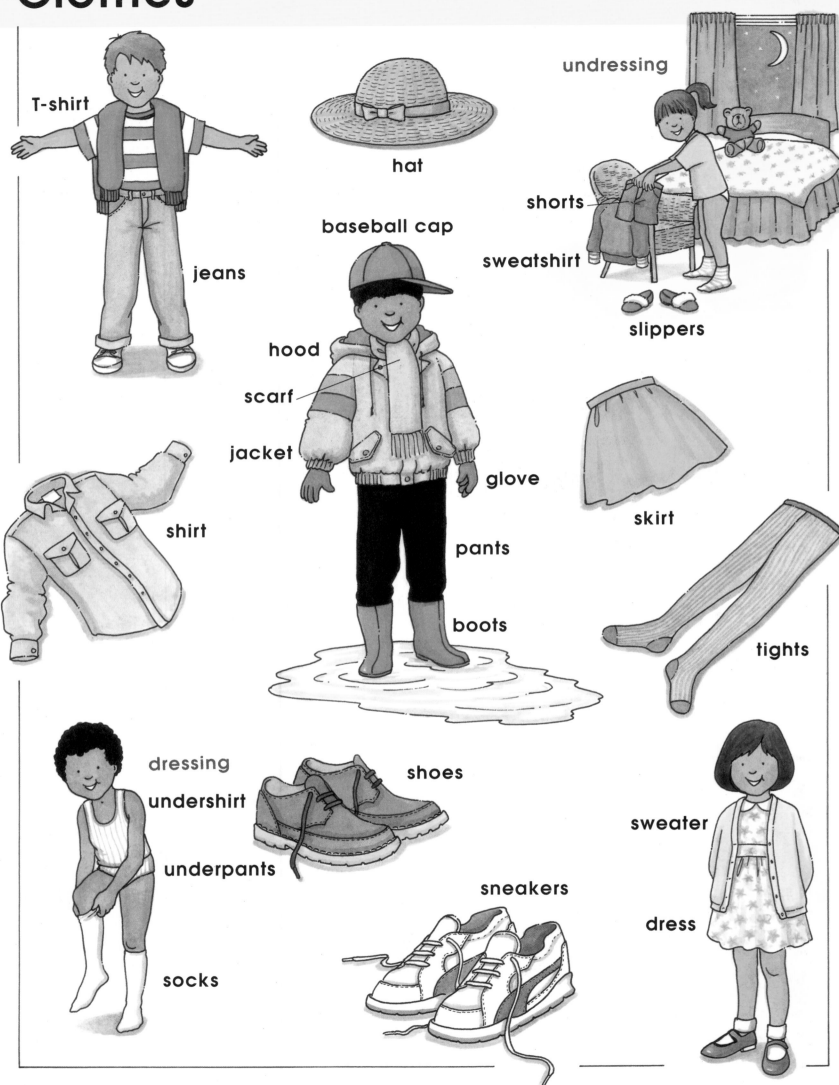

T-shirt

jeans

hat

baseball cap

undressing

shorts

sweatshirt

slippers

hood

scarf

jacket

glove

skirt

shirt

pants

tights

boots

dressing

undershirt

shoes

underpants

sneakers

sweater

socks

dress

# Toys and games

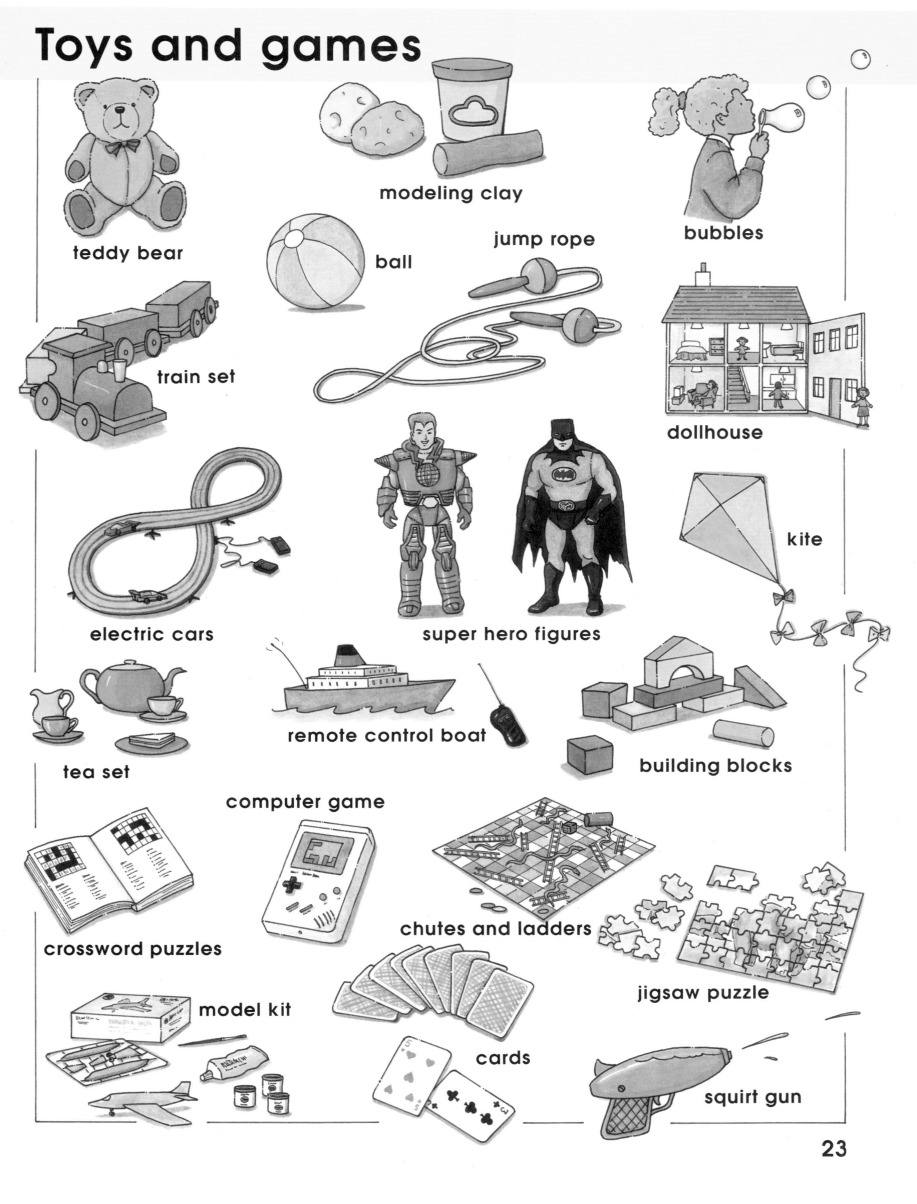

teddy bear

modeling clay

ball

jump rope

bubbles

train set

dollhouse

electric cars

super hero figures

kite

tea set

remote control boat

building blocks

computer game

crossword puzzles

chutes and ladders

jigsaw puzzle

model kit

cards

squirt gun

# At school

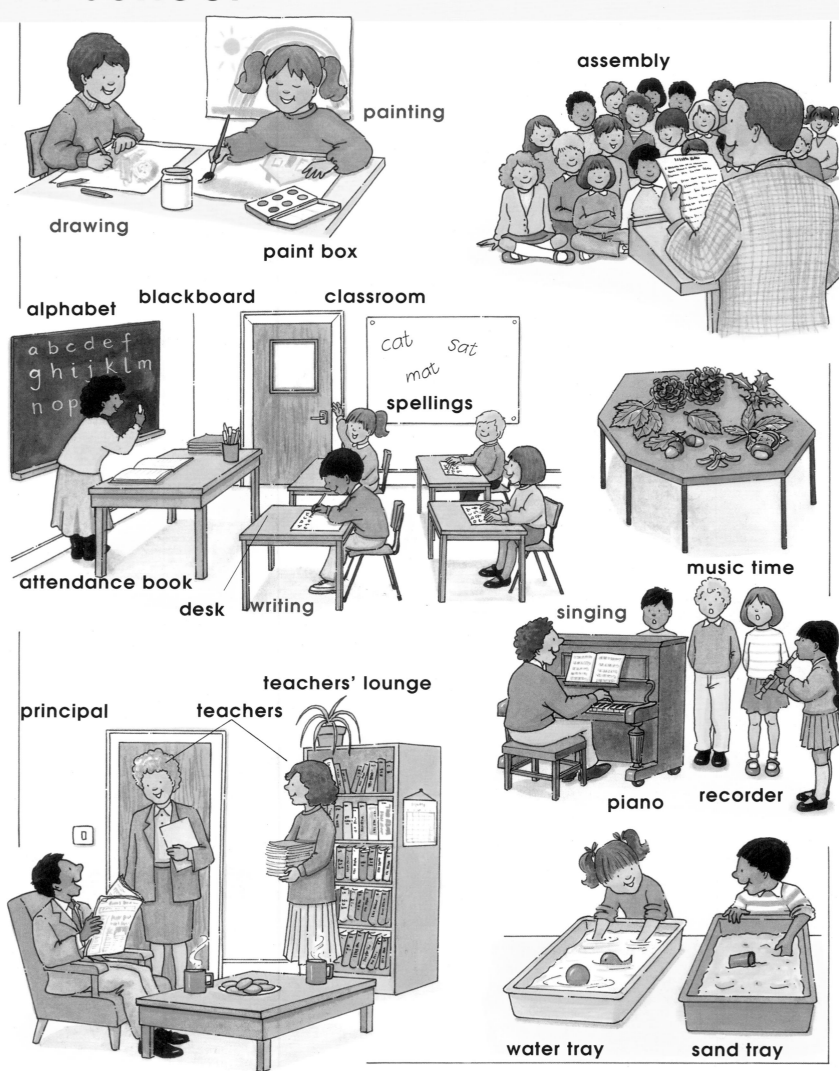

drawing

painting

paint box

assembly

alphabet

blackboard

classroom

cat    sat
  mat

spellings

attendance book

desk    writing

music time

singing

principal

teachers' lounge

teachers

piano    recorder

water tray    sand tray

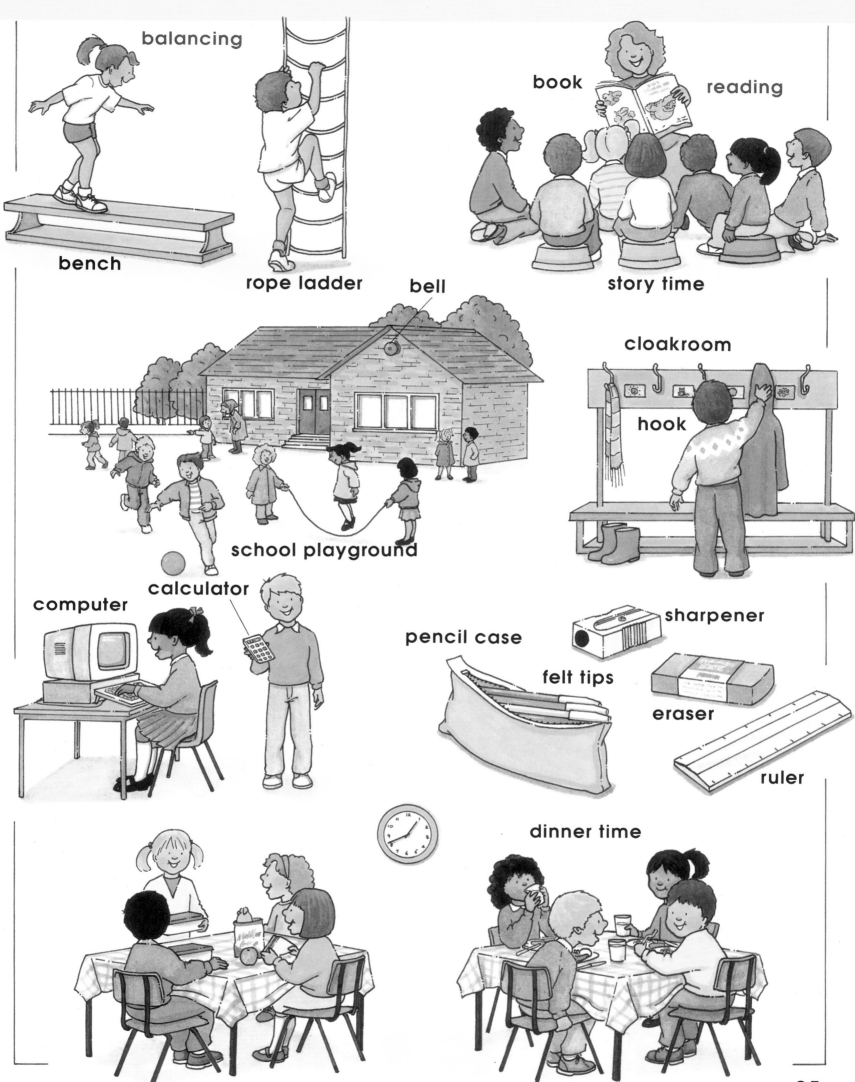

balancing

bench

rope ladder

book

reading

story time

bell

cloakroom

hook

school playground

computer

calculator

pencil case

felt tips

sharpener

eraser

ruler

dinner time

# Shapes and colors

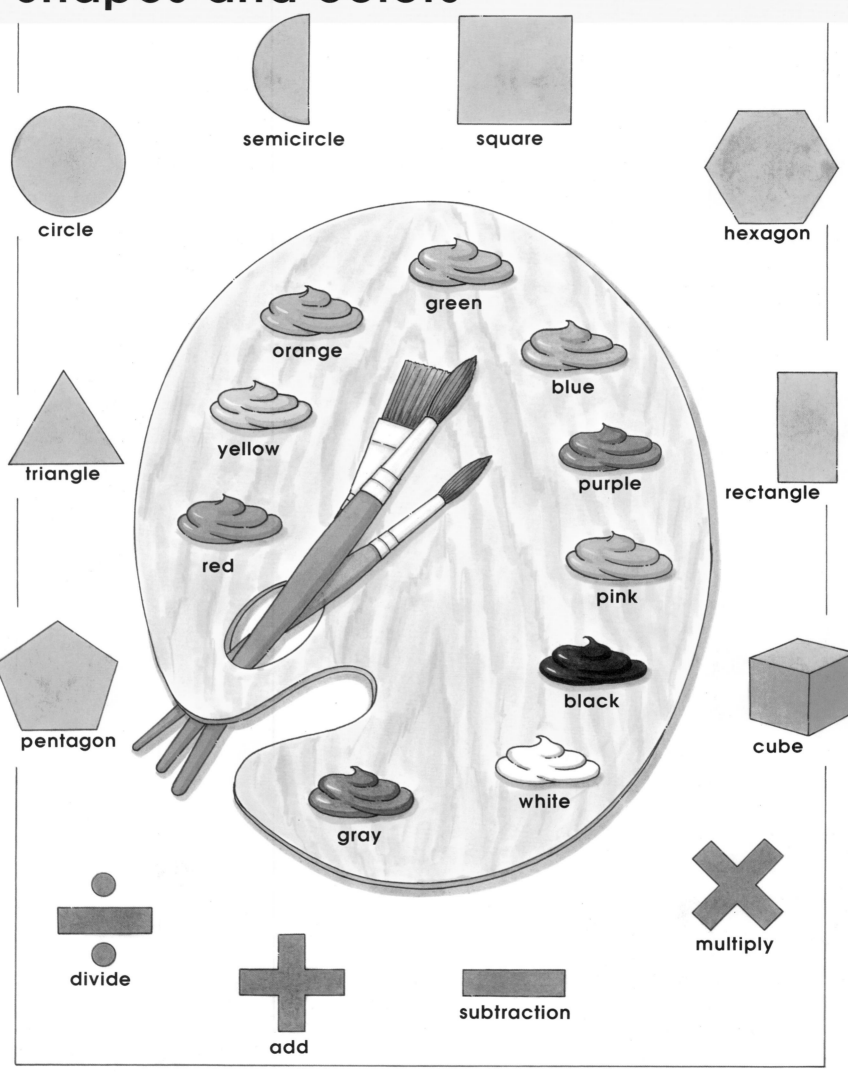

circle

semicircle

square

hexagon

triangle

orange

green

yellow

blue

red

purple

pink

black

white

gray

rectangle

cube

pentagon

divide

add

subtraction

multiply

# Storytelling

elf

fairy

palace

cauldron

witch

toadstool

broomstick

troll

prince

princess

pirate

treasure

cave

knight

King

Queen

dragon

throne

giant

monster

wizard

# Our Earth

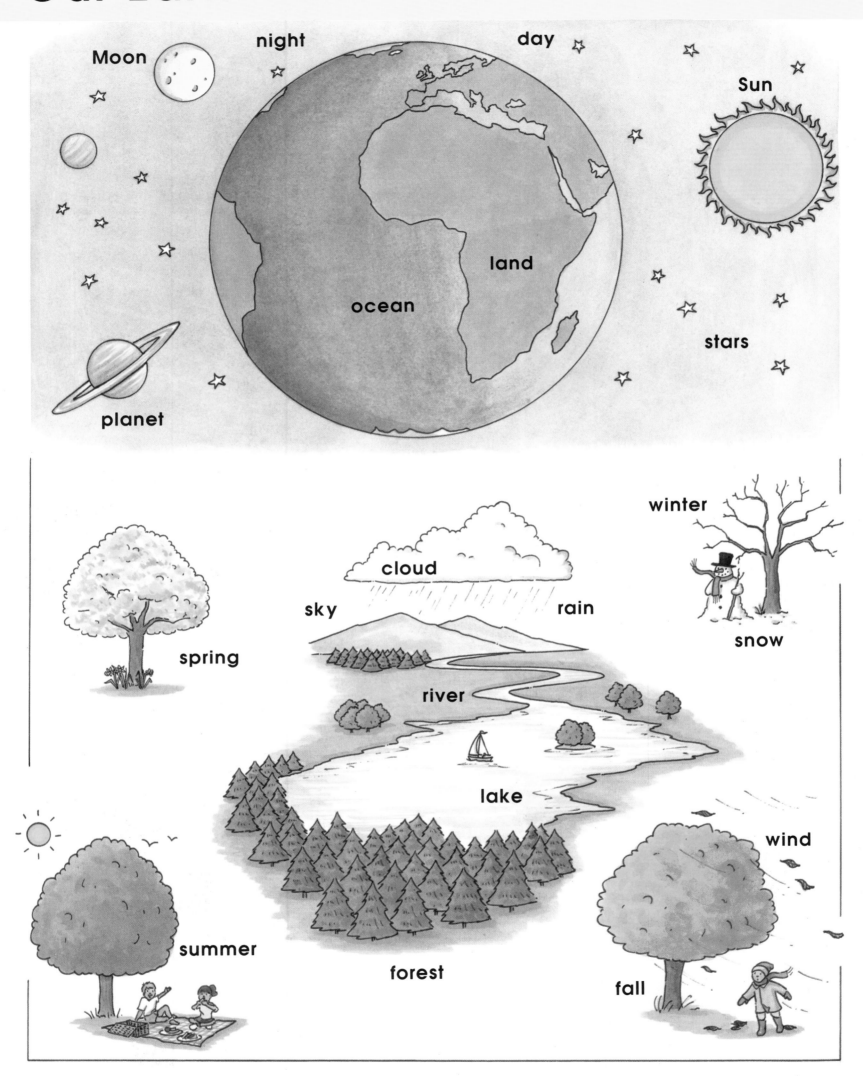

Moon
night
day
Sun
land
ocean
stars
planet

winter
cloud
sky
rain
snow
spring
river
wind
lake
summer
forest
fall

# The words A-Z

The more difficult words are explained. This helps you learn what they mean and how to use them.

## A

 **add** 26

 **adhesive bandage** 21

 **airplane** 11

 **airport** 11

 **alphabet** 24
There are twenty-six letters in the alphabet. Different letters are used to make different words.

 **ambulance** 13

 **ankle** 20

 **answering machine** 17
People can leave a message on this when you are not at home to answer the telephone.

 **ant** 3

 **antiseptic cream** 21
You put this on a cut or graze to help kill any bad germs.

 **apartments** 10

 **apron** 15

 **arcade** 7
A building where you can play computer games or other machines.

 **arm** 2

 **armchair** 17

 **asphalt** 10
The black surface that most roads are made of.

 **assembly** 24
The time when everybody in the school meets together.

 **attendance book** 24

 **aunt** 18

 **automatic teller machine** 12
A machine that gives you your money when you put in your bank card.

## B

 **baby** 18

 **back** 20

 **backhoe** 10

 **backyard** 17

 **bakery** 13

 **baking tray** 15

 **balancing** 25
Walking along a bench or pole steadily so that you do not fall over.

 **ball** 23

 **balloons** 19

 **bandages** 21

 **bank** 12

 **bar code** 14
A mark on things you buy. A computer reads it to find out the price.

 **barn** 5
A farm building used for storing things. Some farm animals, such as cows, live here.

 **baseball cap** 22

 **basket** 2

 **basketball** 6

 **bat** 6

 **bathtub** 17

 **bathroom** 17

 **beach mat** 8

 **bed** 16

 **bedroom** 16

 **bee** 3

 **beehive** 3
A house for bees. Honey is made here.

 **beetle** 3

 **bell** 25

 **bench** 25

**bicycle** 11

 **billboard** 12

 **birdseed** 2

 **birthday cake** 19

 **birthday cards** 19

 **black** 26

 **blackboard** 24

 **blowing** 19

 **blue** 26

 **body** 20

 **bone** 2

 **book** 25

 **bookstore** 13

 **boots** 22

 **bottom** 20

 **bouncy castle** 7

 **bowl** 2

 **bowling** 8

 **bread** 14

 **bricks** 10

 **broken leg** 21

 **broomstick** 27

 **brother** 18

 **brushing** 17

 **bubbles** 17, 23

 **bucket** 8

 **bug jar** 3
A jar used for collecting and examining insects.

 **builder** 10

 **building blocks** 23

 **building site** 10

 **bull** 5

 **bulldozer** 10

 **bumper cars** 7

 **bus** 11

 **bus stop** 12

 **butcher** 13

 **butterfly** 3

# C

 **café** 12

 **cage** 2

 **cakes** 14

 **calculator** 25
A small machine that helps you add and subtract.

 **campsite** 6

 **candles** 19

 **canned food** 14

 **car** 11

 **caravan** 6

 **cards** 23

 **carryout restaurant** 13

 **cat** 2

 **catching** 6

 **caterpillar** 3

 **cauldron** 27
A big pot that witches use to cook in and to make their magic potions.

 **cave** 27

 **cement** 10
Clay and sand mixed with water. It is used to stick bricks and stone together.

 **cement mixer** 10

 **checkout** 14

 **checkout clerk** 14

 **cheese** 14

 **cheetah** 4
A very large spotted member of the cat family. It can run extremely fast.

**cash register** 14

 **chest of drawers** 16

**chimney** 10

 **chopping** 15

 **church** 13

 **chutes and ladders** 23

 **circle** 26
A round shape

 **classroom** 24

 **cliff** 9
Where the edge of the land goes down very steeply to meet the sea.

 **climbing** 6

 **cloakroom** 25

 **cloud** 28

 **cold** 21

 **combine** 5
A large machine that farmers use to cut down and collect their crops.

 **computer** 25

 **computer game** 23

 **concrete** 10
Cement, gravel, and sand mixed with water. It is used to make roads and floors.

 **cookies** 15

 **cooking** 15

 **cottage** 10
A small house, maybe in the country.

 **cotton candy** 7

 **cousin** 18
Your aunt's or uncle's son or daughter.

 **cow** 5

 **crab** 8

 **crane** 10

 **crawling** 3

 **crocodile** 4
An animal like a large lizard that lives in the waters of hot tropical countries.

 **crossing** 12
A safe place to cross the road.

 **crossing guard** 12

 **crossword puzzles** 23

 **cruise liner** 11

 **crutches** 21

 **cube** 26
A square block

 **cupboard** 16

 **cut** 21

 **cutlery** 16

# D

 **daddy** 18

 **dairy food** 14

 **dance** 19

 **dancing** 19

 **daughter** 18

 **day** 28

 **deck chair** 9

 **delicatessen** 14
A store, or a counter in a store, that sells special kinds of cheeses and cooked meats.

 **dentist** 21

 **desk** 24

 **digging** 8

 **dinnertime** 25

 **dishwasher** 16

 **divide** 26

 **diving** 9

 **doctor** 21

 **doctor's office** 21

 **dog** 2

 **doghouse** 2

 **dollhouse** 23

 **dolphin** 4

**door** 10

 **downstairs** 17

 **dragon** 27

 **drawer** 16

 **drawing** 24

 **dress** 22

 **dressing** 22

 **drill** 21

 **drinking** 19

 **driver** 11

 **driving** 11

 **duck** 5

 **duck pond** 5

 **dump truck** 10

# E

 **ear** 20

 **earth** 3

 **eating** 19

 **eel** 4
A fish that is shaped like a snake.

 **eggs** 15

 **elbow** 20

 **electric cars** 23

 **elephant** 4

 **elf** 27

 **eraser** 25

 **eye** 20

# F

 **fairy** 27

 **fall** 28
The season when the days become shorter and colder. Fall comes before winter.

 **falling** 6

 **farm** 5

 **farmer** 5

 **faucet** 16

 **felt tips** 25

 **ferris wheel** 7

 **ferryboat** 11
A boat that carries people or cars across rivers or seas.

 **field** 5

 **fingers** 20

 **fire engine** 13

 **fire station** 13

 **fish** 2

 **fishbowl** 2

 **fish food** 2

 **fishing net** 3

 **flippers** 8

 **flour** 15

 **fly** 3

 **flying** 11

 **foot** 20

 **forest** 28

 **freezer** 16

 **french fries** 7

 **frog** 3

 **front door** 17

 **frosting** 15

 **frozen food** 14
Food stored in the freezer so that it stays fresh for a long time.

 **fruit** 14

 **fruit stand** 13

 **full!** 19

# G

 **garage** 17

 **garbage can** 12

 **garbage truck** 12

 **gas pumps** 12

**gas station** 12

 **gate** 5

 **gerbil** 2

 **giant** 27

 **giraffe** 4

 **glove** 22

 **go-carts** 7

 **goggles** 8
Plastic glasses you wear when you are swimming to keep the water out of your eyes.

 **goose** 5

 **gorilla** 4

 **grandchild** 18

 **grandpa** 18

 **grandma** 18

 **gray** 26

 **green** 26

 **guinea pig** 2

 **gutter** 12
A dip along the side of the road that carries rain water away and down a drain.

# H

 **hair** 20

 **hall** 17

 **hamburger** 7

 **hamster** 2

 **hand** 20

 **happy** 19

 **happy birthday!** 19

 **hat** 22

 **haunted house** 7

 **head** 20

 **headache** 21

 **hedge** 5

 **helicopter** 11

 **helmet** 6

 **hen** 5

 **hexagon** 26
A shape with six sides

 **hill** 5

 **hippopotamus** 4

 **holding** 2

 **hood** 22

 **hook** 25

 **horse** 5

 **hospital** 13

 **hot-air balloon** 11

 **hot dog** 7

 **house** 10

 **household items** 14

 **hovercraft** 11
A boat that floats on a cushion of air over land or water. It normally carries passengers.

 **hutch** 2

# I

 **ice cream** 8

 **inflatable ring** 8

 **ingredients** 15
The different foods you need when you are cooking, such as flour and eggs.

 **intersection** 12

# J

 **jacket** 22

 **jeans** 22

 **jellyfish** 9

 **jet skiing** 9

**jeweler** 13

 **jigsaw puzzle** 23

33

jumping 6

 jump rope 23

 jungle gym 6

# K

 kangaroo 4

 kettle 16

 kicking 6

 king 27

 kiosk 8
A small shed where newspapers or sweets are sold.

 kitchen 16

 kite 23

 kitten 2

 knee 20

 knight 27

# L

 label 14

 lake 28

 lamb 5

 lamppost 12

 land 28

 leg 20

 library 13

 lifeguard 8
Somebody who helps swimmers who are in trouble.

 line 7

 lion 4

 listening 17

 living room 17

# M

 magician 19

 magnifying glass 3

 mailbox 12

 making 8

 margarine 15

 maze 7

 medicine 21
Syrup or pills that make you feel better when you are ill.

 merry-go-round 7

 microwave oven 16
A small oven that cooks food very quickly.

 milk 14

 minibus 11

 mirror 17

 mixing bowl 15

 moat 8
A ditch that is built around the edge of a castle and is filled with water.

 model kit 23

 modeling clay 23

 mommy 18

 money 14

 monkey 4

 monster 27

 Moon 28

 moth 3

 motorboat 9

 motorcycle 11

 mouse 2

 mouth 20

 multiply 26

 movie theater 12

 music system 17

 music time 24

# N

 neck 20

 nephew 18
If you are a boy, your aunt and uncle will call you their nephew.

**nest** 3

 **net** 9

 **newsstand** 13

 **niece** 18
If you are a girl, your aunt and uncle will call you their niece.

 **night** 28

 **nose** 20

 **nurse** 21

# O

 **ocean** 28
A very large area of sea, for example, the Atlantic or Pacific Ocean.

 **octopus** 4

 **office** 10

 **old** 18

 **older** 18

 **oldest** 18

 **orange** 26

 **orchard** 5
A field planted with fruit trees.

 **oven** 15, 16

# P

 **paddling** 8

 **pads** 6

 **paint box** 24

 **painting** 24

 **palace** 27

 **pants** 22

 **parakeet** 2

 **parents** 18

 **parking lot** 12

 **passengers** 11

 **pasta** 14
A type of Italian food made from flour.

 **pastry cutter** 15

 **patient** 21

 **pebbles** 8
Little stones

 **pedal bin** 16

 **pencil case** 25

 **penguin** 4

 **pentagon** 26
A shape with five sides.

 **perch** 2

 **piano** 24

 **picnic** 6

 **pie** 15

 **pier** 8
A building that stands on legs and leads out over the water. It might have a café or an arcade on it.

 **pig** 5

 **pills** 21
The doctor gives you these when you are sick.

 **pink** 26

 **pirate** 27

 **planet** 28
The Earth is one of the nine planets that go around the Sun.

 **plaster cast** 21

 **plate rack** 16

 **playground** 6
Where children can play on things such as tire swings or rope ladders.

 **playing** 19

 **polar bear** 4

 **police car** 13

 **police officer** 13

 **police station** 13

**pool** 16

 **popcorn** 7

 **post office** 13

 **powdered sugar** 15

 **presents** 19

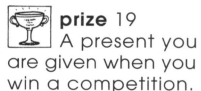 **prince** 27

 **princess** 27

 **principal** 24

 **prize** 19
A present you are given when you win a competition.

 **puppy** 2

 **purple** 26

# Q

 **queen** 27

# R

 **rabbit** 2

 **rain** 28

 **ramp** 6
A slope. Skateboarders use a specially-made ramp to speed up and down on.

 **ranch house** 10
A house that does not have an upstairs.

 **reading** 25

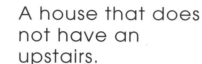 **receipt** 14
A piece of paper that shows how much you have spent.

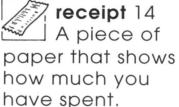 **recipe** 15
This tells you what ingredients you need and how to mix them when you are cooking.

 **recorder** 24

 **rectangle** 26
An oblong shape.

 **red** 26

 **refrigerator** 16

 **remote control boat** 23

 **rhinoceros** 4

 **rice** 14

 **riding** 7

 **river** 28

 **road** 12

 **roller skates** 6

 **roller coaster** 7
A ride at an amusement park where the cars speed along a track that goes up and down.

 **rolling** 15

 **rolling pin** 15

**roof** 10

 **roof tiles** 10

 **rope ladder** 25

 **ropes** 6

 **rotor blades** 11

 **rowing** 9

 **rubber raft** 9

 **ruler** 25

**running** 4

 **runway** 11
A long flat road from which airplanes gather speed and take off.

# S

 **sailing** 11

 **sailboat** 11

 **sand** 8

 **sand castle** 8

**sand tray** 24

**satellite dish** 12
A large circle of metal attached to the side of a house. It picks up television programs that have been broadcast from far away.

 **scaffolding** 10
Poles that are bolted together for builders to climb when they are working on tall buildings.

 **scale** 15
This measures how heavy things are.

 **scarf** 22

 **school playground** 25

 scratching 4

 screaming 7

 **sea** 9

 **seal** 4

 **sea turtle** 4
This looks a little like a turtle. It has flipper-shaped legs and can swim underwater.

 **seaweed** 8

 **semicircle** 26
Half a circle

 **shark** 4

 **sharpener** 25

 **shavings** 2
Fine pieces of wood that are used to keep pets in cages clean and dry.

 **shed** 17

 **sheep** 5

 **shells** 9

 **shelves** 14

 **shirt** 22

 **shoes** 22

 **shopping cart** 14

 **shorts** 22

 **shoulder** 20

 **shovel** 8

 **shrimp** 9
A small animal that lives in the sea.

 **sidewalk** 12
Path which runs along the side of the road.

 singing 24

 **sink** 16, 17

 **sister** 18

 **skateboard** 6

 **skirt** 22

 **sky** 28

 sleeping 16

 **slide** 6, 7

 **sling** 21

 **slippers** 22

 **snake** 4

 **sneakers** 22

 **sneeze** 21

 **snorkel** 8
A plastic tube that you can breathe through when you swim just below the surface of the water.

 **snow** 28

 **soap** 17

 **soccer** 6

 **socks** 22

 **sofa** 17

 **son** 18

 **sore throat** 21

 **sour cream** 14

 **spatula** 15
A wide blunt knife used for cooking.

 **spellings** 24
The right way to spell words.

 **spider** 3

**splashing** 6

 **spring** 28
The season when the days become longer and warmer. Plants start to grow new leaves again.

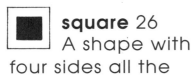 **square** 26
A shape with four sides all the same length.

 **squirt gun** 23

 **stable** 5
A building where horses live.

 **starfish** 8

 **stars** 28

 **steamroller** 10

 **stethoscope** 21
A doctor uses this to listen to your breathing and heartbeat.

 **stile** 5
A step that helps people to climb over walls or fences in the country.

 **stirring** 15

 **stomach** 20

 **stomachache** 21

 **stone slabs** 10

 **story time** 25

 **straw** 2
Dried stalks of plants used to keep animals warm.

 **stream** 5

 **streamers** 19
Colorful strips of paper you decorate the room with when you have a party.

 **stroking** 2

 **sty** 5
A building where pigs live.

 **subtraction** 26

 **sugar** 15

 **summer** 28
The season when the days are long and warm.

 **Sun** 28

 **sunbathing** 9

 **suntan lotion** 9

 **super hero figures** 23

 **surfboard** 9

 **swarm** 3
A lot of bees or other insects flying together in a group.

 **sweater** 22

 **sweatshirt** 22

 **swimming** 9

 **swings** 6

 **switch** 16

# T

 **table** 24

 **tasting** 15

 **taxi** 11

 **teachers** 24

 **teachers' lounge** 24

 **teapot** 16

 **tea set** 23

 **teddy bear** 23

 **teeth** 20

 **telephone** 17

 **television** 17

 **tent** 6

 **theater** 12
A building where people go to see ballets, shows, or plays.

**thermometer** 21
This measures how hot something is. Doctors use a thermometer to measure how hot your body is.

 **throne** 27

 **throwing** 6

 **thumb** 20

 **tidal pool** 9

 **tiger** 4

 **tights** 22

 **toadstool** 27
A fungus like a mushroom. It can be poisonous.

 **toaster** 16

 **toes** 20

 **toilet** 17

 **tongue** 20

 **towel** 9

 **town hall** 13
Where important decisions about the town are made.

 **toy store** 13

 **tractor** 5

 **traffic circle** 12
A circle where several roads meet.

 **traffic lights** 12

 **traffic warden** 12
Somebody who makes sure that cars are parked in the right places.

 **train** 11

 **train station** 11

 **train set** 23

 **treasure** 27

 **triangle** 26
A shape with three sides.

 **triplets** 18
Three children born together at the same time from the same mother.

 **troll** 27
A monster that only exists in fairy tales.

 **truck** 5, 11

 **T-shirt** 22

 **TV antenna** 12
This makes the picture on your television clear.

 **twins** 18
Two children born together at the same time from the same mother.

## U

 **uncle** 18

 **underpants** 22

 **undershirt** 22

 **underwater swimming** 9

 **undressing** 22

 **unloading** 11
When you take objects out of something, for example, boxes out of a truck.

 **upstairs** 1

## V

 **van** 11

 **vegetables** 14

 **video recorder** 17

## W

 **waiting room** 21

 **waking** 16

 **walking** 2

 **wall** 10

 **wardrobe** 16

 **washing** 17

**washing machine** 16

 **wasp** 3

 **watching** 17

 **water bottle** 2

 **water slide** 7
A ride at an amusement park. People sit on mats that shoot along open tubes of water.

 **water fight** 6

 **water hole** 3

 **water wings** 8
You wear these on your arms to help you float in the water.

 **waterskiing** 8

 **water tray** 24

 **web** 3
Spiders make webs to trap flies in.

 **weighing** 15

 **wet suit** 8
This is made of rubber. You wear it in the water to keep you warm.

 **white** 26

 **wind** 28

 **window** 10

 **wings** 3

 **winter** 28
The season when the days are short and cold.

 **witch** 27
An ugly old woman who casts bad spells.

 **wizard** 27
An old man who has magic powers.

 **wood** 10
Trees can be cut up into planks of wood and used to make furniture or other things.

 **wooden spoon** 15

 **woodlouse** 3
A small creature that lives in rotten wood and can curl up into a ball when it is in danger.

 **woods** 5
A group of trees.

 **worm** 3

 **wrapping paper** 19

 **wrist** 20

 **writing** 24

# Y

 **yawn** 16

 **yellow** 26

 **yogurt** 14

 **young** 18

 **younger** 18

 **youngest** 18

# Z

 **zebra** 4

Copyright © 1997
Quadrillion Publishing Ltd

This edition published in 1998 by SMITHMARK Publishers, a division of U.S. Media Holdings, Inc., 115 West 18th Street, New York, NY 10011

8020
Produced by ZigZag an imprint of Quadrillion Publishing Ltd., Godalming, Surrey, England, GU7 1XW

Design: Chris Leishman
Series Concept: Tony Potter

Color separations: RCS Graphics Ltd, Leeds, England
Printed and bound in Singapore
ISBN 0-7651-9262-1

1 0 9 8 7 6 5 4 3 2